Pomeranians 101

Pomeranians 101

✦

Everything You Need to Know About Owning a Pomeranian And Raising Pomeranian Puppies

Kimberly Morin

iUniverse, Inc.
New York Lincoln Shanghai

Pomeranians 101
Everything You Need to Know About Owning a Pomeranian And Raising Pomeranian Puppies

iUniverse books may be ordered through booksellers or by contacting:

iUniverse
2021 Pine Lake Road, Suite 100
Lincoln, NE 68512
www.iuniverse.com
1-800-Authors (1-800-288-4677)

Because of the dynamic nature of the Internet, any Web addresses or links contained in this book may have changed since publication and may no longer be valid.

The views expressed in this work are solely those of the author and do not necessarily reflect the views of the publisher, and the publisher hereby disclaims any responsibility for them.

ISBN: 978-0-595-45077-0 (pbk)
ISBN: 978-0-595-89388-1 (ebk)

Printed in the United States of America

I dedicate this book to
My mom, Gina, my one true inspiration.
Thank you for believing in me and making my dream come true.
You are so beautiful
I love you

Thank you to Dr. Damluji for always believing in me
when I sometimes would not.
I truly look up to you and feel so blessed to have you in my life!
I wouldn't be who I am today without your support

Thank you to Dr. Friesen for caring so much
And for believing in me to follow my hopes and dreams!
Thank you for always being there for me.

Thank you to Dr. "C." Christine Wilson, for caring about my poms
With all your heart
And for always being there when we need you.
You are the best!

My precious Nana
I love you with all my heart
You are my number one and will be forever!

Contents

The Pomeranian

The lively, smart and energetic fellow will win your heart as his vibrancy and spunk capture the world. His royal spirit and unconditional love will lift you high and never let you down! His eager-to-please personality will angelically shine as his devotion to you will last a lifetime. This little being who often thinks he is part human, is known as the five pound dog who thinks he is fifty-five pounds. He is a reliable watchdog that will alarm his owner if need be and protect them with his life; for he is a people dog and people are who he lives for!

Pomeranian Traits

1. Pomeranians are people dogs.

2. Pomeranians are very intelligent dogs.

3. Pomeranians have long full coats.

4. Pomeranians are known to be the 5 pound dog who thinks they are 55 pounds.

5. Poms weigh from 3 to 8 pounds with the exception of a very rare teacup weighing 2 1/2 pounds full grown

6. Pomeranians originated from England with a royal background

7. They are classified as a member of the "Spitz" family

8. Pomeranians do not produce a dog odor.

9. Pomeranians go through what is called the "uglies" faze between four months to one year of age.

Pomeranian Background

Pomeranians originated from England and were considered royalty. Therefore, they have a history of being "royal."

The original Pomeranians' were actually called "Spitz" dogs as a member of the spitz family. Other canines also classified in this "Spitz" category consist of American Eskimos, and Samoyeds. These two breeds look somewhat similar to the "Spitz" Pomeranian as their facial features resemble one another as well as their erect ears and curled up tail. They also have the same type of hair rather than fur. The texture of their coat is dense and full and if it were to become dirty, the dirt would fall off on its own when dry. The "Spitz" Pomeranian also shared a similarity in size to the American Eskimo and Samoyed. They were considered to be of the standard size weighing about 15 to 20 pounds and at that time this was the only size existing for the Pomeranian. Therefore, there were no tiny toys or toys available. It wasn't until many years later that the "Spitz" was bred down in size to these smaller sizes. When a runt of a litter was born, breeders of the "Spitz" Pom would breed the runt with another runt until the tiny toy and toy sizes were achieved. Then, the "Spitz" was given the name "Pomeranian."

Pomeranians became even more popular and they were considered pocket dogs that would go everywhere with their owners. Today, Pomeranians are very desirable and in demand for their size, temperament, and devotion. In fact, right here and now, the "baby boomers" are all wanting a Pomeranian of their own for a companion that they can take with them everywhere.

There are not many standard size Pomeranians that weigh in the 15 to 20 pound range anymore, however some do still exist. Though there are still some standard size Poms being bred, they are not referred to as the "Spitz", but rather now a member of the Spitz family and given the new name of the Pomeranian.

A Pomeranians' lifespan is anywhere from 14 to 18 years of age with little or no aging complications. In the chapter titled "Genetics or injury conditions," it will inform you on a Pom's genetic history.

Choosing Your New Pomeranian

To choose a Pomeranian is to gain a best friend for life! They are full of love, spunk, and inspiration, and live to please you. Their devotion is sincere and unconditional and desire to be around humans, as they are considered "people dogs." When the life changing commitment has been decided to bring a new Pomeranian into your home, you will never regret it. Your heart will feel complete and whole as your new addition to your family brings such joy and warmth to your household.

New Owner's Checklist when choosing the perfect Pomeranian:

1. Always adopt from a reputable breeder or shelter

2. If purchasing from a breeder, always ask to see the parents of the puppy

3. Always observe the environment and surroundings of where the puppy was raised

4. Make sure the puppy has had at least its first puppy shot

5. Always meet the breeder at the breeder's house to visit the litter; never meet at a skeptical location

6. If you don't feel comfortable in a particular situation, don't buy on impulse as there are a lot of reputable breeders out there to purchase your perfect Pom

7. Make sure the puppy is playful and energetic

8. Knowledge about Poms is essential when buying one due to all of the inexperienced "backyard" breeders out there. They will portray false information due to their lack of knowledge in the field of breeding.

9. Know the difference between tiny toy and toy Pomeranians

10. Poms range anywhere from 3 to 8 pounds and most breeders insist that there is no such thing as a teacup Pomeranian. I tend to disagree due to the fact I have produced one so far in my breeding career and at full adult weight weighs 2.6 pounds. He is just as healthy as a tiny toy or toy Pom; he is just miniature in size.

When teacups are born in a litter, all of the littermates are the same size. It is not until about 3 weeks of age you will notice that one is growing at a slower pace than the rest and weighs half of its sibling's size. Teacup Poms are very rare and are not produced very often. They are not considered a runt because they are born the same size as their siblings; they just grow at the rate of a "teacup."

*Note: When observing the Pomeranian puppies parents, it is important to determine their temperment and disposition. One can do so by interacting with the Pom's parents as well as monitering their characteristics around their young. The personality of the parents will reflect on the temperment and disposition of your new puppy. Alert, yet friendly and non-aggressive parents are desirable traits of a well rounded Pomeranian. Bright clean eyes, a clear nose, and a weight fit for their size contribute to the fine health of an adult Pomeranian as well.

An ideal environment for raising Pomeranian puppies would be indoors providing a puppy proof enclosure to ensure safety, with clean and sanitized surroundings.

"Backyard Breeders"

There are many Pomeranian breeders out there, some which are experienced and others that are put under the classification of "backyard" breeders. This term is identified as an irresponsible breeder that has little or no knowledge about breeding Pomeranians. Most of the time these breeders lack the love and well being of the animal but rather are just in it for the money. However, there are wonderful, responsible Pom breeders out there that have the knowledge and expertise in raising healthy and good quality pups. Time and observation in choosing a Pom is essential and by doing your homework, you will find the perfect puppy!

I would recommend avoiding buying a Pom puppy from a pet store. I imply this deeply due to the illnesses and complications I have heard from people that have purchased from a pet store. Sadly but very true, the puppies you see in the pet stores are from puppy mills and usually have various health problems that result in the expense of numerous vet bills. These are not covered by the pet store, but rather strictly out of your own pocket that will not be refunded. I strongly feel that a highly recommended breeder that you have found or have been referred to is the best and smartest way to go. It may take some time in finding your perfect match, but when you do, it will be all the worth while.

Puppy Shots

Puppies need a total of three sets of puppy shots spaced about 3 to 4 weeks apart from each other. The first puppy shot should be administered at approximately 6 weeks of age in which the breeder should complete before the time of the adoption. A Pom should never leave its mother any earlier than 8 weeks old and must be completely weaned prior to the adoption date. A rabies vaccination is to be given by your veterinarian following the three series of puppy shots, however no earlier than four months of age. Fecal samples examined regularly are beneficial to help prevent parasitic illnesses. These parasites found in a puppy or dog's stool are not life threatening but rather preventative medicine to restrict the chances of them reoccurring over and over.

You as the owner can prevent unwanted complications by keeping your Pom up to date on their vaccinations and gaining expertise as you search for a reputable and responsible breeder. With an experienced and knowledgeable outlook in finding the right Pom as your lifelong friend, you will succeed in the perfect match you choose!

Puppy Weight Chart

On the next page I have included an actual Pomeranian puppy weight chart. This is an accurate way to approximately determine the weight your Pom puppy will grow to be as a mature adult. You can, and should take this with you when you decide to purchase a puppy, as you will then understand the difference between a tiny toy and a toy Pomeranian. The instructions of how to read the chart are at the bottom of the second page.

Puppy Weight Chart

Birth	2 1/2 oz.	2 3/14 oz.	3 oz.	3 1/2 oz.	4 oz.	4 1/4 oz.	4 1/2 oz.	5 oz.	5 1/2 oz.
1 week	3 3/4	4	5	5 1/2	6 1/2	7	8	9	9 1/2
2 weeks	5	5 1/2	6 1/2	7	9	10	11	12 1/2	13 1/2
3 weeks	6	7	8	9	11	13	14	16	17 1/2
4 weeks	7	8	9 1/2	11	13	15	17	19	21
5 weeks	8	9	11	13	15	17	19 1/2	22	24
6 weeks	9	11	12 1/2	15	17 1/2	20	22	24	27
7 weeks	10	12	14 1/2	17	19 1/2	22	24 1/2	27	30
8 weeks	11	13	16	19	21 1/2	24	27	29	33
9 weeks	12	15	17 1/2	20	23	26	29	32	35
10 weeks	13	16	19	22	25	28	31	34	38
11 weeks	14	17	21	24	27	31	34	37	42
12 weeks	15	19	22	26	30	33	37	41	45
13 weeks	16	20	24	28	32	36	40	44	49
14 weeks	17	22	26	30	34	39	43	47	52
15 weeks	19	23	28	32	37	41	46	51	56

Puppy Weight Chart								
16 weeks	20	25	30	34	39	44	49	54	59
17 weeks	21	26	31	36	41	46	51	57	62
18 weeks	22	28	33	37	43	48	54	60	65
19 weeks	23	29	34	39	44	50	56	62	67
20 weeks	24	30	35	41	46	52	58	64	70
21 weeks	25	31	36	42	48	54	60	66	72
22 weeks	25	32	37	43	49	56	62	68	74
23 weeks	26	33	38	44	50	57	64	70	76
24 weeks	26	33	39	45	51	58	65	71	78
25 weeks	27	34	40	46	52	59	66	72	79
26 weeks	27	34	40	47	53	60	67	73	80
18 months	2 lb.	2 1/2 lb.	3 lb.	3 1/2 lb.	4 lb.	4 1/2 lb.	5 lb.	5 1/2 lb.	6 lb.

How To Use This Table:
The left-hand column of the table gives the age of the puppy in weeks. To determine it's expected weight when fully grown, weigh the puppy in ounces, look along the line of figure against the number of weeks of its age, and take the figure nearest to the present weight of the puppy. The expected adult weight of the puppy will be that given at the foot of the column in which the figure nearest to its weight occurs.

NOTE: Weights before the age of eight weeks are liable to vary.
This weight chart was taken from a book written by <u>Hilary Harmer</u>. It has been accurate for me to within a 1/4 of a pound give or take a bit.

Tiny Toy Pomeranians

A tiny toy Pomeranian's mature adult weight is from 3 to 5 pounds. Due to the size and weight of tiny toy Poms, it is probably not the best choice for a family of young children. This would apply to children under 8 years of age. Poms of this size can not rough house with children as they may trigger low blood sugar, called hypoglycemia. This occurs mainly if the puppy has not been fed regularly or has been over exerted to the point of dropped blood sugar. If this were to occur in any situation it is crucial to administer a sugar water base like Karo syrup. This is found at any local grocery store and should be kept on hand whenever adopting a tiny toy puppy. Most tiny toys will never have a bout of hypoglycemia, but it is always good to be well prepared for this low blood sugar situation. Another healthy nutritional supplement that can be given regularly to maintain a steady blood sugar, is a product called Nutri-Cal. It can be found at most pet stores and is packaged in a long tube like box. Dogs love the taste and it is a great daily nutritional supplement.

An ideal situation or environment for a tiny toy Pom would be a family with older mature kids that fully understand the fragility of these tiny toys. Especially as puppies it is important to watch your step as they like to get right under your feet. Also, it is crucial that your tiny toy Pom never have the opportunity to jump off a bed or couch, as their bones are fragile and they may break a leg. With careful observation, your tiny toy Pom may sit with you on the couch as long as assistance is given when needed to get down.

Elderly people are quite fond of tiny toy Poms because of their size and weight. With tiny toys weighing between 3 and 5 pounds, these little one's can sit on their owner's lap for longer periods of time without the pain of unbearable weight on their legs. People with sore legs or muscles benefit from tiny toy dogs as they are less strenuous to carry or hold.

Always make sure that you see the parents of the tiny toy Pom before you purchase it, as many breeders will sometimes mistaken the difference between a tiny toy and a standard size Pom. It may be an unintentional mistake however it can be prevented by your knowledge of what to look for and what you want in a Pom. To help ensure your decision in choosing a tiny toy Pomeranian, one can predict the size of their new puppy mainly by how much he or she weighs. From the time a Pom puppy is about 6 weeks old their weight at this age establishes their weight at adulthood. This the most accurate and effective age to use the puppy weight chart provided on the previous page. A tiny toy Pomeranian should weigh less than two pounds at 8 weeks old as this would classify him as reaching an approximate adult weight of three to five pounds. A three to five pound Pomeranian is classified as a tiny toy, and a six to eight pound Pom is catagorized as a toy size. Standard size Pomeranians are usually known to be ten pounds and over.

A tiny toy Pom is a wonderful addition to your family and with the right environment, care and situation a successful longevity are in store for you and your new best friend. Tiny toy Poms should be kept indoors as they are classified as indoor lap dogs. They are so small that they could very well get hurt by wild animals such as hawks, or foxes, or even coyotes. With monitored playtime outside, they can satisfy their activity level and get just the right amount of beneficial exercise. As with all toy breeds their size pretty much determines the indication of always being indoor dogs.

Tiny toy Poms hold their own and no matter how big or small, their hearts touch us so deeply that they become a part of us forever. The next chapter continues with the next size up from tiny toys. Toy Pomeranians will win your heart as well, because *"Angels are just Pomeranians with wings!"*

Toy Pomeranians

Toy Pomeranians wrigh from 6 to 8 pounds full grown. The only difference between tiny toy and toy Pomeranians is their size. All Pomeranians are good natured, loyal dogs that are devoted to humans and live to please their owner's.

The toy size Poms are not as fragile as the tiny toys, however monitoring your youngsters with any toy breed dog is beneficial. The average weight of a toy breed at 8 weeks of age is about 2 pounds. Pomeranians usually develop their mature adult weight at approximately 6 months of age. By the age of 6 months it is an appropriate age to have your Pom spayed or neutered. Most veterinarians will not perform this surgery earlier than this age.

Toy Pomeranians, as well as tiny toys, love to be with you. They enjoy traveling with you and going on car rides. They also do very well with other pets and enjoy the companionship of other Pomeranians. If you work long hours during the day, an ideal situation would be to have two Poms so they could keep each other company during their alone time. Particularly in a confined area, especially during the puppy stages, with bedding, toys, food and water. This provides security for your Pom as well as your own peace of mind for prevention of your puppy's safety. Pomeranians do get lonely if left in the house alone for long periods of time, so having a friend for them is something to consider. Your toy Pom will adapt to your household rather quickly and will follow you everywhere! If desired they love to sleep in bed with you, however if you as the owner decide to crate train your young puppy for sleeping that works just as well. Poms do quite well in dog carriers and some even like to wear clothes! A Pom's love is unconditional and will be devoted to you for life. Remember, *"Angels are just Pomeranians with wings!"*

Teacup Pomeranians

Teacup Pomeranians are few and far between. They are very rare and one can not predict the breeding of producing a teacup Pomeranian. The thing about teacups is that you do not know he or she is a teacup until the litter of pups is about three weeks of age. All of the puppies in the litter are born the same size and it is not until about three weeks of age that one of the pups starts growing at a slower pace. This puppy is not a runt because if it were a runt there would be a significant size difference at birth that would continue throughout puppy hood. The weight of the teacup from three weeks on was half the weight of his siblings. Since the growing rate of the puppy is not noticeable until a few weeks after delivery, the classification is known as a "true teacup." This does not happen in every litter and in fact it rarely happens. This same sequence of events occurred when I got my two teacups. They were both from separate litters and happened a year apart from each other. They both had different parents and one litter had five puppies in it and the other had only two. I didn't know they were teacups until they were both approximately three weeks old. They were perfectly healthy puppies and they were definitely completely developed. They were just miniature puppies classified as teacup Pomeranians. I still keep in touch with my very first teacup that I sold to a wonderful lady and sure enough, fully matured at 8 months old he weighed 2.6 pounds.

A teacup puppy's mature adult weight is from 2 to 4 pounds and should weigh about ½ a pound at 8 weeks old. Also a teacup will weigh and look half the size of its siblings.

Pictures of "Teacup" Pomeranians at 8 weeks old
A true "Teacup" Pom should weigh less than one pound at 8 weeks old!

A true "teacup" weighing 12 ounces at 8 weeks old!!

Another true "Teacup" weighing only 9 ounces at 7 weeks old!!

Nutrition

A well balanced nutritional diet is an essential part of a Pomeranian's life. Achieving this nutritional diet should begin at the start of early puppy hood. One brand of dog food I highly recommend is called Royal Canin. Royal Canin is a nutritionally complete and balanced dog food that meets the needs for all toy breeds. Its natural ingredients with balanced protein and fat levels provide optimal energy to maintain a healthy weight.

Royal Canin mini puppy number 33 is the ideal food for growing puppies ages nine weeks to ten months. With its easy digestion, it increases protein digestability which leads to better obsorbtion of vital nutrients. It also includes DHA brain development which supports early cerebral development. Its easy to chew kibble size, is perfectly suited to the jaw of the small breed puppy.

Royal Canin mini adult number 27 is a well balanced diet for all toy breeds ages eleven months to eight years. With enhanced palatability, its flavor combination satisfies even the most demanding palate. Essential fatty acids, amino acids and vitamins combine to protect the coat. Sodium tripolyphosphate and specialized kibbles help to reduce dental plaque and limit tarter formation.

I highly recommend both Royal Canin mini puppy number 33 and mini adult number 27 for all Pomeranians. I am very satisfied with the health and well being of my Pomeranians as their daily diet consists of Royal Canin.

Note: One can find Royal Canin at Petco and Petsmart.

These are just some healthy guidelines to help start you on your way. There are many foods out there and by studying a variety of them, you are sure to find one to suit your dog's liking.

Nutri-Cal

Nutri-Cal is a high calorie nutritional supplement that provides an immediate boost in a puppy or dogs' blood sugar. I recommend using Nutri-Cal as a part of your Pomeranians daily nutrition although they may not be prone to low blood sugar (hypoglycemia), it would work as a leveler to keep it well balanced. Nutri-Cal is based as a sugar water paste that all puppies and dogs crave the taste for. You can find Nutri-Cal at Petco, Petsmart, and most other leading pet shops.

Training

When we think of training a Pomeranian, a few key factors come into mind.

1. POTTY Training

2. Obedience

3. CONFINEMENT

So let's start at the very beginning. To simplify things in perspective, all toy breeds are the most difficult to potty train than any other dog breed. Why? There is really no one certain answer to this problem but rather recommendations to make the situation easier. Although it may take a little longer to potty train your Pom, they will learn so don't give up!

Potty Training

Puppy pee pads are a wonderful alternative to going outside to potty. Pee pads can be found at a variety of pet stores and locations selling pet supplies. These pads are specially designed for puppies and dogs that use an attractive scent that attracts them to go on it. They are super absorbent to protect your carpet and hard floors and are a great solution for indoor potty training. Always praise your Pom with joy and excitement and reward him/her with a small irresistible treat. The treat that you choose for this moment of happiness should only be used for this particular type of rewarding. Your Pom will automatically distinguish the cause and effect of the good thing he did and the reward he receives! I use them for my Poms and have been very successful in doing so.

Crate training is a positive reinforcement for potty training. Your Pom will catch on fairly quickly with this method as dogs do not like to go to the bathroom in their sleeping quarters. The crate should be big enough for them to stand up and turn around, yet not so big that they have room to go potty. If placed in the crate every night around the same time after they have had a chance to go potty, they should hold their urine and bowels until the morning. At that time you should immediately take them to where you want them to go potty and then praise them with love and happiness. Also, the crate should not have food or water inside. Dogs actually like the security of a crate and most of the time they freely go to it at bedtime. Honestly speaking, I happen to prefer the pee pad method rather than crate training as I find the puppy pee pads have a greater effect on the puppy's learning development.

If outside pottying is chosen, frequent outside potty breaks are necessary. Young puppies tend to have to go to the bathroom about 10 to 15 minutes after each meal they eat. At this time I recommend taking your puppy to the door repeating the words, "potty time" or something of that nature. By consistency of a certain noise or behavior every time during potty training, your Pom will relate that sound to having to go potty. Before long it will be a positive habit for your Pom and in result will be a consistent daily routine. They will adjust to their owner's schedule as well. Giving praise is important and very rewarding for your pom. A certain treat given only at the time of going potty is beneficial as your Pom will combine the praise, treat and pottying together and will succeed to please you. As long as repetitive consistency is formed and rewarding praise is given, your Pom will learn in no time. Remember practice makes perfect and patience is a virtue.

Obedience

Obedience should start at an early age as a puppy's disposition sets the stage for an adult temperament. Some puppies tend to have bad habits whether it's chewing, biting or barking. All three of these things can be prevented or corrected with the help of you, the owner. It is important to never hit or hurt your Pom if he or she misbehaves, but rather to use adamant reinforcement. A tap on the nose with the word "NO" is a persistent way to state your point followed by a ten minute time out by themselves if needed. Being confined and separated completely from the situation is a successful technique. Usually by adulthood a dog is pretty much set in their ways. Positive correction and discipline strengthens the bond between a dog and their owner. The main characteristic one should always remember when training a Pomeranian is, you are in charge. Pomeranians are an extrelemy intelligent breed and with guidelines and boundaries, their obedience willl be fulfilled to the best of their ability.

When it comes to leash training your Pom, getting them used to walking on a leash is the first step. Once familiar with it they tend to behave quite well, however due to their size they can not walk too far of a distance. Always make sure water is provided as their blood sugar can drop quickly from dehydration.

Confinement

Confinement is a positive reinforcement from the time you bring your new puppy home, and all through the stages of puppy hood. An example of confining your Pomeranian would consist of a human baby playpen, to a wire pen made for dogs, or even a big crate. Although I mentioned using a small potty training crate that is just the right size for sleeping, a bigger crate can be used for confining your pom when you are unable to watch them closely. I highly recommend confining your Pom through puppy hood at times when you are not home so they do not have the opportunity to get into things in your house without your observation. It is always a good idea to not let your puppy have full run of the house in the beginning anyway, due to injury or destruction to material things. Inside the larger crate or playpen, I recommend warm bedding on one half, a pee pad on the other half and little bowl of food and water on the bedding side. They will usually go potty on the pee pad as they do not like to soil on their bedding.

Barking

Pomeranians are NOT excessive barkers. Well socialized puppies that are well cared for and loved portray the best reputation that most Pomeranians hardly ever bark.

Pomeranians are the 5 pound dog that thinks he is 55 pounds. This makes him the best little watch dog. He will bark when the door bell rings or if he hears an unfamiliar noise but with reassurance that he can stop, he will obey. Pomeranians will never bite and are definitely not aggressive. An uncommon situation of a Pomeranian that has been abused in the past may make him bark or nip at people but with professional training you can hopefully break that pattern.

Grooming

Brushing

Pomeranians should be brushed about once a week to maintain a healthy and full coat and to eliminate knotting and matting. A brush with firm bristles is ideal to effectively and efficiently comb your Pom all the way through.

Bathing

Since Pomeranians do not produce a dog smell, it is unnecessary to bathe your Pom very often. Once every couple of weeks is sufficient and if desired, professional groomers will do it for you. There are many local groomers that provide excellent grooming services to meet your needs.

Sanitary Cuts

A sanitatary cut is the name given to trimming the hair around the Pomeranian's anus. I definitely recommend this consistent trim as in doing so you will save yourself many messy clean ups! A good pair of dog sheering scissors will do or even electric clippers for dogs. If you don't feel comfortable doing this yourself, your veterinarian or local groomer will be happy to assist you.

Nail Clipping

Before you clip your Pomeranians nails yourself, please have a veterinarian or groomer show you the correct way. It is not a hard technique to learn, however if inexperienced, you may quick your dog. Quicking your dog will make his nail bleed a little and he may let out a yelp, but he will be fine by applying pressure to the quicked part of the nail. Practice makes perfect and the best way to learn something is to do it hands on. Your veterinarian or grooming salon will be happy to do this service for you if you would feel more comfortable than learning yourself.

Tear Stains

All Pomeranians have tear stains; however you only happen to see them on light colored pom's. Washing can reduce the reoccurrence of staining considering it is not consistent. If tear stains become persistent and are progressively getting worse, please seek veterinary attention as there could potentially be an underlying cause.

Double Coat vs. Single Coat

A Pomeranian with a Double Coat
A Double coat means that their coat is Massive!!

A Pomeranian with a Single Coat
A Single coat means that their coat lies more flat on their back and is not as full.

The Pomeranian "Uglies"

Picture of a Pomeranian going through the "Pomeranian Uglies"

In my opinion "ugly" is not the best word to describe what I would call the adolescent faze of a Pomeranian!

During puppy hood, a Pom puppy will go through a period of looking quite straggly and sometimes not so pretty. It is a well known trait for the Pomeranian and yes every pom will go through it! The "uglies" or "adolescent" faze can start as early as 10 weeks of age and carry through to as long as a Pom's first birthday. The classification of this faze is described as losing their puppy coat as they transition into their gorgeous, massive adult coat. A Pom puppies coat will start to thin and look a little uneven and also somewhat shorter. By one year of age a Pom should be completely through adolescence and have developed into their mature adult coat!

Genetic and Injury Conditions

Pomeranians in general are quite healthy and do not have many genetic health problems. As with most dogs there are a few factors in Poms, however they are not life threatening and most can be prevented.

Dental Hygiene

Poms are prone to bad teeth. They tend to produce plaque and tarter continuously and if not treated, their teeth will decay and become infected. The preventative medicine for tooth decay is to brush your Pom's teeth regularly with supplies from a reputable pet store or vet's office. You can also have your Pom's teeth professionally cleaned by your veterinarian. This is a simple and safe procedure that can be done about once every two years. By doing this it will prevent plaque and tarter build up from reoccurring and in result obstruct the chances of tooth loss. Your Pom's breath will smell refreshed and he or she will feel better as tooth decay is painful and no Pom should have to go through that.

Retained Deciduous Teeth

Pom's can develop what are called retained deciduous teeth. This is understood as never losing some of their baby teeth. The adult teeth come in just fine however it leaves a double tooth formation known as a retained deciduous tooth. This does not cause them pain and it usually only occurs in a couple of teeth. The baby teeth can be removed if they are retained, to prevent an uneven jaw bite as well as food deposits in between the two teeth. Most likely a veterinarian will take the residual teeth out at the time of a spay or neuter. However, this may be done at anytime as it is a simple procedure.

Patella Luxation

A rare problem in Pomeranian's that is undetermined by veterinarian's whether to call it genetic or injury, is called patella luxation. A luxating patella is a knee cap that pops in and out of its joint rotating to the side of the knee. This occurs in the hind legs consisting in one or both knees. There are 4 levels of intensity in this condition with level 4 definitely requiring surgery to correct it. Being at level 4 is quite painful and the knee cap is permanently rotated to the side and unable to pop back. At this point the Pom can not put any pressure or weight on this leg and therefore is restricted from most daily activities. Surgery is insisted to correct this problem and in result can continue a normal lifestyle free of pain when healed. There is no determination as to classify this condition as genetic or injury as neither of the two has evidence to prove each other wrong. Most Poms have luxating patella's, however they are usually levels 1 through 3 and do not require surgery. The knees may pop in and out but usually will never get to the point of permanently staying out therefore are not painful like level four.

Poms can injure themselves quite easily due to their size. It is important to not let them jump off high surfaces as if they land wrong they may break a bone. Their legs are fragile especially as a puppy, so careful monitoring of your Pom will prevent an unfortunate situation.

Collapsed Trachea

Due to the Pomeranian's small size, they can be prone to have what is called a collapsed trachea. This may NOT be a life threatening condition; however it is aggravated by heat or allergies in one's house hold. They may develop a dry hoarse cough as their collapsed trachea takes effect due to its narrowing airways. To help avoid these circumstances it is recommended to keep your Pom cool in the midst of high heat temperatures and to evaluate the underlying cause of your Pom's possible allergies if affected by a collapsed trachea.

Reversed Sneezes

Reversed sneezes are quite common in Pomeranians and they sound like a raspy snorting noise. This can occur by over exciting oneself during play time, or eating and drinking too fast, or even just out of the clear blue. This situation is not life threatening and it may take just a few seconds for your pom to catch his/her breath. They are not affected in any way by reversed sneezing as it is just a normal aspect of a toy breeds' life.

No Dog Odor!

Poms do not produce a dog odor. There is something in their glands that prevents them from producing the smell that most dogs have. It is a wonderful aspect in the Pomeranian that also is true for the American Eskimo and the

Samoyed. All three of these dogs are from the "Spitz" family and have similar traits.

As long as you are familiar with these particular conditions your awareness can prevent and prolong the life of your beloved Pomeranian. The genetic history of a Pom is not life threatening but rather indications of preventative medicine to a happy pain free life. With regular vet visits and keeping your Pom up to date on their vaccinations you will have a healthy Pom.

Colors of Pomeranians

The most common colors of the Pomeranian include:

- orange
- orange sable
- red
- red sable
- black
- cream
- cream sable
- sable

The rarest "exotic" colors include:

- blue
- blue and tan
- blue sable
- black and tan
- chocolate and tan
- chocolate
- chocolate sable
- Tri-color (black, tan and white)
- white
- beaver
- lavender

-parti

-merle

Parti's are two colors consisting of mostly white.

-Irish parti's are the most common of the parti color as they have more colored markings than they have white.

-The next in line would be the spotted parti which consists of more white along with colored spots on their back and face.

-The rarest of the parti color is called the piebald parti. This consists of mostly white with one patch of color on their head and one or no spots on their back or tail.

Parti's are very rare and desirable no matter what their color of markings are.

Some parti's have a mask of color on their face with a white strip along the center of their forehead. This is called a white blaze.

The many colors of the parti include:

-black parti

-cream parti

-sable parti

-orange parti

-red parti

-blue parti

-Tri-color parti (chocolate and tan, or black and tan markings with white all over)

-chocolate parti

-Beaver parti

-lavender parti

-merle parti

Lavender colored Poms have a mauve tint to them along with the same color nose, eye lids, lips and paw pads. Lavender Poms are very rare and difficult to produce.

Blue colored Poms have a grayish blue hue to them with a blue nose, lips, eye lids and paw pads. Blue Poms are always born with a blue nose that stays blue forever. They are also very rare.

Chocolate Poms have a chocolate nose, lips, eye lids and paw pads.

The sable coloring on an orange, red or cream Pom stands for the black highlighting distributed throughout their coat.

Chocolate sable indicates a light undercoat with chocolate highlights.

The merle color is among the newest and rarest of the Pomeranian. The merle gene is the dilute pigment of the color black. Meaning wherever there is the color black, whether visible or in the bloodlines, it is diluted by the merle gene.

The different colors of the merle include:

-merle-blue merle

-sable merle

-merle parti (all parti colors with the markings diluted with the merle gene)

-chocolate merle

-lavender merle

-beaver merle

-cobalt blue merle (blue undercoat with dark blue spots)

Blue, beaver, lavender and fawn are all colors of the dilution black. These colors bred together will produce like colors.

The beaver color is among one of the rarest and consists of a dark beige color. They have a liver colored nose as well as lips, eye lids and paw pads.

Breeding Pomeranians

First we come to understand the most important questions we must ask ourselves before our impulse jumps right into breeding Pomeranians. As with any hobby or business we run into bumps in the road that will only better ourselves to keep striving for our highest goals and achievements. These particular questions we should ask ourselves will lay a steady and mature path for the amazing journey you are about to take!

1. Do you have the time and dedication to care for and raise your Pomeranians?

2. Do you have the appropriate space and environment to house your Pomeranians?

3. Are you financially stable enough to afford a substantial number of vet bills that come along unexpectedly, and to also pay for the care and well being of your beloved Pomeranian(s)?

These three questions are definitely not to steer you away from breeding Pomeranians, but just to enforce the time and devotion you will need to become a successful Pomeranian breeder. Pomeranians are people dogs. They desire to be around people and are extremely devoted to their owners. Just as you will be dedicated to them, they will reciprocate that same love right back to you!

With any pet, unexpected vet bills can arise out of the ordinary, however it is very important to be financially prepared for those unexpected expenses.

Now that we appreciate the basic understanding of these three questions, let us proceed further with the true beauty of breeding Pomeranians!

Choosing Your Breeding Lines

When choosing a Pomeranian that you are considering or planning to breed in the near future, it is very important to use these 10 guidelines before you purchase the perfect pom.

1. Never buy from a pet store

2. Always make sure you see the parents

3. Know that a Pomeranians' mature adult weight is from 3 to 8 pounds.

4. When breeding or showing your Pomeranian(s) they must be breeding/show quality (there is a difference between breeding/show quality and pet quality). Breeding/show quality poms will have massive coats, short compact bodies, and perfect color and marking formation.

5. Look at the environment of where the puppy(s) was raised and what kind of care he or she received.

6. Make sure the puppy(s) have AKC papers (without AKC papers on both the mother and the father pom you can not register the litter of puppies with AKC). AKC stands for American Kennel Club. These papers assure the new owners of your puppies that they are definitely acquiring a purebred dog. Also, having AKC registered litters is beneficial to breeders' because the profit of the puppies they sell rises due to the fact they are papered. I recommend using AKC, however there are other affiliations you can use. Just remember if you buy a puppy or adult pom to breed and they have AKC papers, always keep your line of breeding poms with AKC. For example: your poms should have the same kind of papers to avoid confusion when registering a litter of puppies.

7. Make sure the puppy or dog you are buying to breed in the near future has had at least their first puppy shot (if acquiring a puppy), and is up to date on all vaccinations (if acquiring an adult pom).

8. Make sure the puppy or dog is alert, healthy and active, yet has a friendly and affectionate personality. I myself breed for temperament and disposition so all of my dogs have outstanding personalities.

9. It is important to always get a slightly bigger female to breed to your male stud dog. This way the puppies will not grow to be bigger then the

mother can pass. If the male pom is substantially larger than the female pom problems will arise into a probable cesarean section. It is moderately okay to have the male and female poms' equal in size when breeding them, however it is recommended to have the male pom slightly smaller to avoid unfortunate situations.

10. Always ask questions when buying a puppy or adult pom to breed in the future. Promise yourself you will gain full knowledge and confidence in the field of breeding Pomeranians before you start producing litters of your own. This will benefit you and your beloved poms for years to come. Also, never give up. There are always life lessons and learning techniques in any hobby or business and overcoming each and every obstacle will only make you stronger and more confident as a person. You can succeed in anything and everything you set your mind to and accomplishing your goals and dreams are the passions that make life worth living!

Beginning in the Breeding World of Pomeranians

The true beauty of breeding Pomeranians is the art of knowledge and love we give these amazing animals, and sharing with others our expertise of what we are so passionate about. The importance of understanding the animal kingdom through Pomeranians is the education we learn so we can enhance the breeding world of Pomeranians!

Becoming knowledgeable in the field of breeding Pomeranians is the main factor in successful puppy raising. I want to share my expertise with beginning Pomeranian breeders, to help them on their way to becoming a successful Pomeranian breeder.

Let us start at the very beginning of the amazing world of breeding Pomeranians!

Mating Seasons

To reduce the risk of unexpected complications it is best to not breed a female pom under the weight of 4 pounds. I would recommend breeding females in the 5 to 7 pound range.

Female Pomeranians usually come into their first heat cycle anywhere from 6 months to 1 year of age. You should always skip their first heat cycle as they are still pups themselves and there could be health concerns for both the mommy and her babies. Approximately 6 to 8 months after their first heat cycle they proceed into their second heat cycle. This is the ideal time to mate them to a male pom. I would suggest that the male pom be smaller in size compared to the female. As long as the male is no bigger than the female he is mating with there should be no problem of the babies growing too big for the mother to deliver. Female poms usually come into heat about every 6 months but can come in up to one month early or up to two months late.

Occasionally you will see a drop of blood or two when your female pom comes into heat, however she usually keeps herself quite clean during this time. A female pom is in heat for a total of about 4 weeks. During the two weeks of her period where she is actually bleeding, she most likely will not let the male get to her. The male will try and she will refuse because she is not at the peak of ovulation. You will also notice the female pom's vulva is noticeably swollen to about double its original size. By the time the female has finished her period; she will start flagging her male and will be willing to mate. The male pom will mount the female and they will tie together as the male's penis swells inside of her. They can not and will not separate for several minutes to this tying affect. Don't be alarmed if the female squeals. Whether it is the female's first time of mating or if she is experienced, this reaction is perfectly normal and it usually happens this way every time.

When you notice your female pom is coming into heat it is crucial that you keep her and the male you have chosen to mate with her in a confined area or room until her mating season has been completed. I also recommend from my own personal experiences that you only have the male mate with her for three days in a row. Although the male and female can mate everyday for a whole week it is best to restrict it to a total of three consecutive days. I imply this strategy due to puppies of mine that have been born prematurely. If one or two of the puppies were conceived on the first or second day of ovulation and the last one or two puppies conceived at the end of that week, the first two pups are going to be full term at the time of delivery and the last one or two are going to be premature. If you condense the mating to a series of three day in a row you will avoid the unfortunate circumstances of a puppy born premature.

A male's sperm lasts for 24 hours and a female's egg ovulates for a total of 36 hours. Depending on the connection of the sperm and egg meeting at the same time during their individual hours of survival, three days of mating gives a reassuring value of time for conception to take place.

A litter of puppies can have multiple fathers so it is very important to confine your female to one particular male at the time of mating and to not let any other males get to her in the time of heat. You only need one male stud per 5 or 6 females that you are planning to breed. A male will know exactly when a female is in heat as his nose will be glued to her behind. Males can sense a female in heat up to one mile away. Just like women living in the same house, multiple females housed in the same environment will most likely come into heat on the same schedule. If your females had separate living arrangements from each other, they would most likely stay on their own individual pattern.

When breeding Pomeranians or in this case any breed of dog, line breeding is permissible and inbreeding is inexcusable. Line breeding can be beneficial as having a line of Pomeranians that are somewhat related further back in their pedigree, will keep perfecting the line of puppies that they will produce. Inbreeding is when you breed a mother to a son or a father to a daughter or even a brother to a sister. This is when problems like birth defects present themselves at the time of the birth of the puppies. It is sad but some people just don't know the harm they are doing when they inbreed. Breeding half sisters to half brothers or an Aunt to a nephew or an Uncle to a niece is a form of line breeding. This is okay and will not result in any harm what so ever. In fact it is a way to keep perfecting a pom's generation for years to come.

A female pom should only have two to three litters in a row before she needs to take a break. Depending on the size of her litters, your determination on whether she should rest after two or three is your judgment call. Poms usually have between two and four puppies in a litter with the exception of a couple more depending on the size of the female. Breeding a female pom too often can result in a concern to the mother's health and complications can arise in her pregnancy and delivery. Also, the quality of the puppies begins to downfall if the mother dog lacks the opportunity to regain her strength in between litters.

A Pomeranian's Pregnancy

The gestation period for a female Pomeranian is 58 to 65 days. During a female pom's pregnancy, she will form an even stronger bond with her owner and want to be with them even more than before. There are three trimesters in a female pom's pregnancy. The first trimester her hunger pattern will increase. The second trimester her hunger pattern will start to subside and she will want to rest more frequently. In the third trimester during the last couple weeks of her pregnancy, the babies will start moving and you can even feel them kick inside her stomach. Her hunger pattern will increase drastically and it is a good idea to start her on a canned food once or twice a day. This gives her just the right amount of added nutrients counteracted with the dry food she is on. I recommend Science Diet adult canned food. You can find this at any Petco or Petsmart. Her belly will become noticeably large in size and she will begin to sleep quite often to gain strength for delivery. During her entire pregnancy it is beneficial to provide a daily multiple vitamin for your pom. This will enhance the nutrients she needs to stay strong and healthy prior to her delivery. You can purchase a multiple vitamin for dogs at a local pet store. A complete and balanced diet is also important to maintain a healthy body for the mommy and her young. I recommend a dog food called "Royal Canin." It has all natural ingredients with hardly any fillers and provides a well balanced nutritional diet for every pom. You can find this dog food at Petco or Petsmart.

A couple of weeks prior to the mommy's delivery, it is important to introduce a confined place in your home where she will feel safe having her babies there. I recommend a bedroom in the house where not a lot of traffic is entered by it, providing a whelping box where she will have her babies. The whelping box can be as simple as a cat litter box or as personal as something you make for her. It should be big enough for her to lie down in it as well as room for her to nurse her young following the delivery. About a week before her due date it is a good idea for her to start sleeping in the room where she will have her babies. This will regain her confidence and familiarity of where she can safely deliver her babies.

Always mark each date on your calendar of when the female and male mated. It is very important to keep a record of this so you know when her first due date should be. Then count approximately 63 days from the first day of mating and that will be her probable due date. The average gestation for a pom is 63 days, however give or take a day or two depending on her actual day of conception.

Silent Heat Cycles

It is quite common for female Pomeranian to have silent or skipped heat cycles. This indicates that her body is refusing to let her get pregnant at this time to allow her to regain strength for future pregnancies. In the Animal Kingdom, the female Pomeranian's body knows what she can handle and what she can not in the present day and time! She will then attempt to show now signs of a heat cycle and therefore the male will not be attracted to her powerful scent. The male will follow no interest to mate with this particular female.

Silent heat cycles differ from false pregnancies in the sense that with a silent heat they skip their cycle completely, and with a false pregnancy, she does come into heat indicating a true but false pregnancy.

False Pregnancies

It is definitely not uncommon for a female Pomeranian to have false, or the correct term known as "Suddo" pregnancies. A female Pom's body knows and determines when she can and can not get pregnant. Just because a person may breed her with a male, doesn't necessarily mean she is going to follow through with a pregnancy. However, you may think she is pregnant due to the same symptoms and signs she will have as if it were really true. The female may still produce milk and precede with all of the preparation signs as if she were in the beginning stages of labor. She may indicate these signals but will never begin to bear down and push because technically there are no babies for her to deliver.

Labor and Delivery

It is important to know and understand the 4 signs that determine the birth of the babies' is approaching fast. By taking a rectal temperature of your female pom twice a day for one week before she is due, you will find out what her normal temperature should be. When you notice her temperature dropping to the low 99's to the 98's your female pom should have her babies within 24 hours. This is the first accurate sign that delivery is nearing. The next three signs include panting, nesting and refusing to eat anything that particular day. When these indications are clear to you, it is crucial that you are able to stay at home with her until she delivers safely. Do not hover over her and make a big fuss during the early signs of labor and delivery. Just keep her confined to her quiet whelping box and check on her every few minutes without being in her presence consistently. When you first notice her start to bear down and push, it is then beneficial to stay in the room with her to make sure she has a successful delivery. By monitoring this stage closely, keep an eye on the clock. If your female pom has been pushing for 30 minutes and there is no sign of a puppy, it is time to seek assistance from your veterinarian. In this case she might need some occitosin to help induce the labor. The last resort would be to deliver the puppies by cesarean section. This would be an unlikely situation as long as the puppies were not too large for the mother to pass.

It is always a natural instinct for a mother dog to know what to do to care for her young even if it is her first time. My recommendation is to not step in as the breeder and do everything for the mother but rather to be there just in case human assisting is required. In the animal kingdom, the mother dog's natural instinct takes over and their protective instinct let's you know they want to do everything themselves. You as the breeder will know if the mother is tired due to their lack of interest. At that point in time it is okay to step in and help her out.

There are three stages of labor in a female pom. The first consisting of heavy panting and nesting. The second stage begins the contracting and pushing, and the third stage results in the delivery of the puppies. Each pup is separated into their own sack and placenta when they are inside of their mother. When each individual puppy is born the mother must break each sack and cut each umbilical cord. She will due this willingly and diligently without harming her young. The mother dog will also clean up after herself and it is important to let the mother eat each one of her baby's placentas as this helps her milk drop so she can start nursing in an effective manner.

After the first baby is born, each baby after that usually delivers within minutes of each other. The average sequence of time between each pup is 15 to 20 minutes apart. However don't be alarmed if it takes 45 plus minutes between each puppy during delivery.

Following the delivery of all the puppies in that litter, the mother's panting will come to a stop and she will be washing and stimulating her new babies. The mother dog will be very hungry considering she has not eaten since she refused her food the day before. A plate of canned food is desired along with a big bowl of water to regain her strength and blood sugar. Along with her food a calcium tablet should be administered once daily to keep her milk supply flowing and also to stabilize her calcium level as long as she is nursing. You can buy a bottle of calcium tablets either at your veterinarian or any local pet store. If need be a human tums tablet will do. Nutri-Cal is a high calorie nutritional supplement that enhances the endurance of the mother's body strength. Nutri-Cal should also be given once or twice daily for about a week following delivery by squeezing a quarter size amount onto your finger for her to lick off. All dogs love the taste and it is a great blood sugar booster. It can also be found at Petco and Petsmart.

One of the most important key factors following the delivery is to not hover over the puppies or move them at least for the first 24 to 48 hours of life. This time is crucial for the allowance of the mother and her young to bond and if they are handled by the breeder too often in the beginning, the mother might think you are going to harm them. As a result she may suffocate them herself as smothering them close makes her feel they are protected by her. Intentionally she may not mean to suffocate them but as she takes fear into precaution in hiding them under her, the result is tragic. Please only check on the mother and babies periodically to make sure that the mother has food and water and that the babies are finding nipples to nurse. Other than that let the mother dog be the mother reassured that her natural instinct knows exactly how to care for them.

My Own Experiences

As we encounter experiences in life whether they are good or bad, joyful or upsetting, we always find a life learning lesson at the very end of that journey. There is always room for growth in whatever we do and accomplish in our lifetime and overcoming hardships makes us stronger and more experienced as human beings. These next few real life experiences are all facts of my life and what I have encountered so far in my field of breeding Pomeranians.

Pomeranians are considered to be called the "heartbreaker breed." Due to their small size there are definitely going to be more complications when breeding them. My experiences are not to discourage you from breeding them but rather to prepare you for the unexpected and give you the guidance you need to never give up.

Pancreatitis

1. When my very first female Pomeranian got pregnant I was informed by a reputable specialized veterinarian to only have her diet consist of puppy food. Yes puppy food has a lot of nutrients yet it also has an extremely high amount of fat intake. I listened whole heartedly to that individual advice knowing that I wanted to do everything the right way. Everything was going smoothly all throughout the pregnancy and delivery and it wasn't until my female's baby was completely weaned that I saw a change in the mother. As I continued to feed her puppy food, she suddenly started vomiting and couldn't keep anything down. She them started having diarrhea. I was very concerned and rushed her to my vet. My vet soon diagnosed her with Pancreatitis. Pancreatitis is the disease of the pancreas. It is the underlying factor for consuming too much fat in one's diet. I was forced to feed her strictly broiled boneless skinless chicken breast mixed with white rice as her sole meal. This would help control the bout of vomiting and diarrhea caused by the Pancreatitis. After a couple of weeks on just chicken and rice she was then switched to a special dietary food called W/D. This is mainly for dogs with pancreatitis that has no crude fat and should be given as the only source of food for life. Even on this food for life, a dog with pancreatitis can still have bouts of the

illness. However it is not life threatening and can be controlled continuing this W/D food and not consuming any fat in their daily diet. Never feed a puppy food as the significant source of a pregnant dog's diet, but rather to continue her daily food intake as always with added nutrition specifically for a dogs; not puppies.

Premature Births

2. Premature births are definitely a tragedy to bear and hard to overcome the situation. I always knew that a female and male dog can mate everyday for a whole week if they wanted to, however I didn't realize the puppies would conceive at different times. Depending on the conception date of when the eggs become fertilized, the puppies toward the end of the week are going to be born premature compared to the one's that conceived days before hand. Always breed your female no more than three days in row to reduce the risk of premature babies. These babies are sometimes stillborn (born already dead) or sometimes only live for a few hours after delivery. Breeding a female three days in a row ensures that the puppies are all conceived about the same time therefore by the due date of the female, all of the pups are full term and fully developed.

The Mother's Natural Instinct

3. The mother dog's natural instinct lets her know if a puppy is a perfect puppy or if there is something wrong whether it is internally or visibly. I had a very tragic experience not to long ago where one of my females (a rather large pom) gave birth to seven babies. She had no problem breaking their sacks or cutting their umbilical cords, except I was alarmed to see on two of the puppies she pulled their intestines out when cutting their umbilical cords. I immediately rushed both puppies to the emergency vet and wanted to do everything possible to save them. With their little immune systems not even stabilized yet by the milk of their mother, the vet said there was no chance they would make it through the surgery, and replacing intestines is very painful. These puppies only weighed two ounces each which is the average weight if a newborn pom, so I questioned why the mother would do such a thing. The vet's response indicated that the mother's natural instinct told her that there was something internally wrong with these pups to begin with and weren't strong enough to make it in this world. With this professional explanation I began to remember that the mother didn't even mind when I took them away from her. I then began to realize the true beauty of the animal kingdom and the phrase known as "the survival of the fittest." It all started to make sense and from that moment on I new all of my breeding

mother's had amazing intuitions in their ability to know things that we as humans do not and can not always see.

Selling Puppies

4. When the time comes to start selling the litter(s) of puppies that you raise, please be extra cautious in the people that inquire about your puppies. There are a lot of shady and skeptical people out there that are not trustworthy and are sometimes criminal prone. I want to share a devastating experience with you about my first encounter of selling a puppy. I had just completed weaning my very first puppy that I had successfully raised and decided to place an ad in the Union Tribune classifieds. I only had one puppy in that litter and she was pure white which is very rare for a Pomeranian to snow white. I was well prepared to screen the people that were interested in her as I new she must go to an exceptional home. One afternoon I received a phone call from a nice young couple that wanted to come see her. I set up an appointment with them at my house later that afternoon. They came over and liked the puppy and were holding her. The wife of the man holding her said she was going to go to her car to get her cell phone. I was in the kitchen with the gentlemen as he was holding the little puppy. He asked me if he could see her AKC papers. They were right behind me on the kitchen counter so I turned around for two second to grab them. I turned back around and he was gone. My heart jumped in my throat as I ran to the front door. It was wide open and I heard foot steps running down the driveway and their car sped off. I started screaming as my mom came running. Being my first time selling any puppy I did not suspect any problem and had never had anything stolen from me ever. I then realized his wife went to the car to get it started and on her way out she left the front door wide open so her husband could escape without me catching up to him. We filed a police report but since they were parked at the bottom of our long driveway we were unable to retrieve their license plate number. Basically they got away with stealing my puppy and I am sure they were going to sell her to make a profit for themselves. Even though they didn't have her papers, I found out from a dog lawyer that it is easy for them to fake papers. I also found out from the dog lawyer that these criminals make a living stealing puppies from innocent people. Please be so careful when having strangers over to your house and always have somebody there with you observing and helping you at all times. Pick one room in the house preferably close to the front door and have everything you need to sell the puppy right with you on hand so you never lose sight of your puppy and the potential buyer. Always listen to your intuition as well and if you don't like the sound of someone on the phone don't

hesitate to put them off as you have to feel comfortable all the way around. Also, don't feel bad if you have to turn people away because you don't like the situation your puppy might be going to. It is in your hands as the breeder to do whatever you feel is the right thing to do and don't regret it. Your gut is always right so never question it and go with your first impression. The people might be mad but just remember this is your personal property and your puppies that you care so deeply about. I myself have turned people away before because I have not felt comfortable with the situation and environment my puppy would be living in. They were mad and stormed out, but at least I knew I had done the right thing for my puppy and my peace of mind. Never be intimidated by people and always have your wits about you and you will be fine. I have never had a problem like this since and I never will because of my precautions and practice of ruling out the good and the bad in people.

Dominant males

5. Knowing which one of your male Poms has the more dominant disposition is very important for your awareness when breeding Pomeranians. When a female comes into heat all of the males you have will want her. They will even fight to kill each other over a female in heat. A dominant male will start the fight until they all chime in as a pack and tear a smaller more innocent male apart until they kill him. I had an unfortunate experience around Christmas time in the year 2005. I had recently acquired a male that I rescued from another Pomeranian breeder that could not keep him anymore. He was a sweet dog, and we didn't expect any problem. Until one day the dominance issue broke out. My mom and I were outside in the front yard when we heard terrible barking coming from inside our house. My mom flew inside to find our little teacup orange male almost unconscious and bleeding terribly. The rescue dog was continuously pecking at him to the point of almost killing him. It was all over a female that had just come into heat that I was not aware of yet. We rushed our little teacup immediately to the vet where he was put on an iv and thoroughly examined. He was then rushed to the emergency vet where they had to perform emergency surgery due to his displaced intestines. He spent one full week in the emergency hospital where we visited him three times a day and we weren't going to let him give up. Three times the doctor's called to prepare us he wasn't going to make it through the night. He proved the doctor's wrong and made a full recovery. Our vet bill totaled $7,000 but we didn't care because all we wanted was for our little guy to survive. We were very fortunate in this situation as many people might not be. We found a really good home for the rescue dog and made sure from then on we

did not have any dominant males. Please be aware of when your females come into heat. Check their vulva's for swelling often, and signs of being on their period, and also please be in tuned to your males if you have more than one. They will try to kill each other over a female and unfortunately situations like mine have not turned out so promising. Always keep the two pom's you plan to mate confined to an area where no other males have the opportunity to come in contact with them. I want to reinforce this to every Pomeranian breeder as I don't want the same thing to happen to you, like what happened to me.

Tube Feeding a Litter of Pomeranian Puppies

My second breeding female named Apache that I had acquired from a friend and reputable breeder, was 6 weeks pregnant at the time I brought her home. Pregnant females tend to become very affectionate and loving during this time, and it wasn't too long after I got her that we became bonded. Apache was so devoted to me as she was my shadow! I would rock her in my rocking chair and my love grew so strong for her that I knew she would be mine forever. At the very end of her pregnancy something didn't seem right. Apache started vomiting consistently and she started contracting but no pushing. I rushed her to my vet and at that time they did a couple of tests. One being a progesterone test to see if she was at the peak of delivery. With no hesitation she was in need of an emergency cesarean section. I was so nervous for my baby girl and her pups. As the doctor took her back to the operating room, I stayed in the front office nervously waiting. What was minutes seemed like hours and then the doctor came out with promising news. Four puppies were just born and were breathing on their own. There were two girls and two boys and mommy was doing well also. I got to see the babies while mom recovered for a couple of hours. Before I knew it we were on our way home. My good friend Kellie had met me at the vet to help me take everybody home. When we arrived home we got mommy and her babies upstairs to the nursery to get them situated. Then something went terribly wrong. Apache's eyes started to roll back in her head and she became unresponsive. Kellie decided to rush her back to the vet while I stayed and got the babies acclimated. Kellie was gone a few minutes and arrived back home without Apache. She told me Apache was going to stay there awhile to get fluids intravenously. A short time after Kellie was home I received a phone call from my vet. Apache had suddenly gone into cardiac arrest and didn't make it. I was devastated. These puppies did not have their mother so what was I going to do? My vet then met me at her office with the four pups and told me that the only way to try and save these babies was to tube feed them.

NOTE: Tube feeding is a huge and risky responsibility but it is their only chance of survival. Proper demonstration of tube feeding is required before an individual attempts to tube feed newborn puppies on their own.

Bottle feeding is even more risky than tube feeding as they can aspirate which will lead to death. Aspirating is when they ingest too much formula too quickly and it gets into their lungs which then suffocates them.

I was willing to take on this major responsibility as I wanted to save them for Apache. I was taught the correct way to tube feed by my vet and picked it up quite naturally. I had to tube feed them by putting a long tube down their throat that went directly into their stomach and then inject a formula filled syringe into the opposite end of the tube. Every four hours around the clock I was tube feeding them following pottying them with a warm wet cotton ball just like the mother would stimulate them to go potty in her own way. As the puppies grew I had to remeasure the tube according to each puppies size marking the tube so I would know how far to put the tube down each puppy. I also had to keep measuring the amount of food per serving according to the weight of each pup. Sleeping in between feedings and sterilizing tubes and syringes after every meal was difficult yet at the same time an amazing experience I will never forget. I knew my dog Apache would want me to save her pups and I knew she was guiding me every step of the way. This challenging yet rewarding experience helped me grow stronger as a person to live my life to extreme success. To watch these little lives grow stronger everyday because I became their mother, gave me such a feeling of accomplishment and I now know I can conquer anything that life brings me. I saved little helpless innocent lives that wouldn't have had a chance if it weren't for my devotion to their survival and well being. My little angels grew up and were placed in forever loving homes as they are perfect little puppies thriving for life. I will always remember being the mother to these puppies as I hold the memories dear forever. I will also never forget their biological mom, my baby Apache, as she will always hold a special place very close in my heart!

Facts You Need to Know About Breeding Pomeranians

1. You shouldn't start breeding your female Pomeranian until she reaches her second heat cycle.

2. Male Pomeranian should always be smaller than the female when breeding or at least the same size as her. Ideal weight for a breeding female is 5 to 7 pounds. Ideal weight for a breeding male is 3 to 6 pounds.

3. Gestation for a female Pomeranian is 58 to 65 days.

4. Nutrition is very important including a well balanced diet with added multiple vitamin everyday. Calcium is also essential following the birth.

5. Do not give your pregnant female too much fat intake as a result of feeding too much puppy food. It will cause pancreatitis.

6. Only breed your female three days in a row during her heat cycle.

7. Keep your female(s) in heat confined to one area so only one male of your choice mates with her.

8. Give your breeding female(s) resting periods after they have had two or three litters in a row.

9. Know how to assist with the delivery if need be.

10. Let the mommy pom be the mom and don't hover over the babies even though they are so cute. Also, it is crucial for at least 24 to 48 hours after delivery do not handle the puppies. As a result the mother may become over protective and smother them.

The Merle Gene

The Merle gene can be a complicated factor in the world of breeding. It is very important for breeders to understand every aspect of the Merle gene before producing Merles takes place. Researching and educating yourself about Merles will take time and dedication, however, with complete knowledge you will be successful in the near future. In this chapter you will begin to learn everything you need to know about breeding Merle Pomeranians!

The Merle gene is a dominant gene therefore it only takes one parent to produce Merle puppies. You can NOT breed a Merle to a Merle due to the fact that the Merle color is a defected color of the dilution color black and breeding two together will produce major defects. You can also never breed a Merle to a white or cream colored Pom. Breeding a Merle to a Merle, or a Merle to a white or cream, will cause serious birth abnormalities such as blindness, deafness, and even tragedies such as pups born with no eyes and/or ears. As you can see this is a serious matter and should be taken very delicately. When you breed a Merle to a non-merle you will be successful. Even though the Merle gene is a defect of the diluted color black, the Merle dog is not defected at all. A Merle Pom bred to a Parti (two colors consisting of mostly pure white) is okay. Even though there is white, no defects will be presented as the dog is not solid white in color. So basically you can not breed a merle to a merle, or a merle to a solid white or a solid cream.

When a merle is bred to a non merle, half of the puppies in the litter will be merle and the other half will be merle factored. Merle factoring means they don't have any visible signs of being a merle but one of their parents is a merle, therefore they carry the merle gene. Merle factored Pomeranians should also never be bred to a merle. Some breeders think that by breeding a merle factored to a merle they will get all merle puppies in one litter. The truth of the matter is that even though the merle factored pom does not indicate any signs of being a merle, they are definitely considered a merle due to the fact that one of their parents is a merle.

Also, a merle factored pom often portrays the name of a cryptic or phantom merle. The cryptic or phantom merle is still considered a merle and all new owners/breeders must be aware of this trait before attempting to breed. If you are planning to breed a cryptic or phantom merle, it must always be bred to a non merle also excluding the color white or cream. This will avoid all defects and abnormalities of the merle and merle factored puppies.

It is very crucial to acquire the factual information about merles before an individual decides to breed them. Merle's can be a complicated gene if one is not properly educated in the field of breeding them. However, with great expertise and complete understanding, Merle's are a delightful new addition to the line of Pomeranian colors.

This is a Blue Merle Pomeranian

A Mother Pomeranian "Blowing" Her Coat after Having a Litter of Puppies

Mother Pomeranians will grow their "Blown" coat back when they come into heat again!!

All mother Pomeranians go through a period of what is known as "blowing their coat." This occurs when their puppies reach the age of about 8 weeks old. The mother's hair starts to come out in clumps and brushing their excess undercoat out is necessary. This is their bodies way of expressing the end of their successful pregnancy. The mother's coat will begin to grow back over the next couple of months and by their next heat cycle it will have completely grown back in.

The Heart Breaker Breed

Pomeranians are known as the "heartbreaker" breed. Due to the size and weight of the Pomeranian, it is true that there are going to be unexpected tragedies when breeding them. Unfortunately it makes no difference whether the female is 3 pounds or even 8 or 10 pounds. The delicate newborn puppies are sometimes not strong enough to survive in this world. The average weight of a newborn Pomeranian is between 2 ounces to 5 ounces. Sometimes a puppy will be born that looks perfect to the human eye but internally they are just not a perfect puppy. We then need to come to the understanding of the fact known as the Darwin's Theory, Survival of the Fittest. This term interprets who can fight for survival in this world and who is just not strong enough to survive. A puppy may only live for a few hours as it fights to stay alive, however nature determines the destiny of this puppy. Just remember if you lose a puppy or two in a litter it is nothing you did personally. It must not have been a perfect puppy and nature will take its course. We can't control the universe and we must have faith that nature knows what is best. Losing puppies is heart breaking and it is never easy to go through it but if we remember Darwin's Theory of Survival of the Fittest, we will understand the life of the animal kingdom.

Stud Services

Studding out your dog can be a very serious matter. Before you consider using your male Pomeranian as a stud, please contact your veterinarian, as he/she will inform you regarding all of the possibilities that can occur. Unfortunately there are many sexually transmitted diseases passed from a male to female dog and vice versa. It is highly beneficial to you and your pet to become educated about stud services and the details entailed. A potential traumatizing experience I encountered could have turned disastrous, however it became resolved. From now on I will never stud out my male Pom again. Please contact your veterinarian to learn more about all of the particulars and most important for the safety and well being of your pet.

Contracts

The importance of a contract when a sale of a puppy is in progress is to protect you as the seller, and to inform the new owner(s) of the rules and regulations before the sale of the puppy is completed. There are some people out there that may take advantage of you if a contract is not in place at the time of the sale. Coming from my own experience, please save yourself the distress and know your boundaries in the beginning. This reassures the buyer that the sale is final requiring a signed contract from both parties. A formative contract from the seller to the buyer, states that both parties will never abide by the terms of agreement.

Weaning a Litter of Pomeranian Puppies!

As the puppies grow and reach approximately 4 weeks of age, they are starting to develop teeth. The mother starts to feel rather uncomfortable as her offspring nurse and the pups are also at the point of needing more than just mom's milk! When the puppies reach the age of 4 and 4 ½ weeks old it is an appropriate time to start introducing some solid food to their diet. This should be introduced very gradually so that the mother still feeds her young in between feedings.

First you need to start with a puppy canned food. I highly recommend Science Diet puppy canned food. Mixed with the puppy canned food should be a puppy milk replacer. I definitely recommend the brand "Esbilac." This is a puppy formula that replaces the puppies' mother's milk when she is not feeding them. The instructions of the amount per serving of this formula are on the container of the powdered Esbilac. It is important to read the directions of how to mix the powder with water to ensure the proper amount is given. Next scoop out a couple of spoonfuls of the puppy canned food and chop it up real fine. Then pour some puppy formula over the canned food making sure that the texture is very thin and runny. You want the first few meals that you introduce to the puppies to be watered down because they are new to whole foods and may possibly choke on chunks of food in the very beginning. As the puppies get used to the liquid based food you may then start to thicken each meal little by little until they are just on the canned food itself. Also, dry food may be introduced about the time the puppies are 5 weeks old. At this age they are definitely starting to teeth and like the feel of the dry kibble on their gums. They are also old enough to chew and digest this form of food very easily. When the puppies reach about 5 ½ to 6 weeks, the mother should only be in their pen with them for sleeping. By 7 weeks the pups should be completely weaned and eating solid food.

At 6 weeks of age, the puppies should receive their first puppy shot given by your veterinarian. At this time your vet will perform a full physical exam to make sure that each puppy in the litter has a clean bill of health. This also reassures the new owners purchasing your little babies the kind of quality they are getting.

Also, you as the breeder become more reputable to your name and people admire the responsible person you truly are.

At 8 weeks the puppies should be ready to go to their new forever homes. Screening your buyers and making sure that your puppies are going to exceptional homes will give you peace of mind as to where they are going and who they are going to. With your puppies adopted and everything done the right way, you may compliment yourself for your success and accomplishment. Your devotion and dedication are admirable and respected because breeding Pomeranians is not an easy thing to do. You are a success and your Poms will thank you for years to come!!

The life stages of a newborn Pomeranian puppy!

2 days old!!

One week old!

2 weeks old!

4 weeks old!

8 weeks old!!!

Parasites

Fleas and Ticks (External)

All Pomeranians develop fleas and sometimes ticks. To help prevent these bugs from manifesting themselves on your pom's skin, a flea and tick medication is needed. I recommend the brands Frontline or Advantage. These are two well known name brands that veterinarians use and distribute. Please do not use generic brands found at your local store fronts as they do not have the same effect and can be harmful to your pet. Frontline and Advantage can and should be administered once every 30 days. To apply you squeeze the tube of formula directly onto the dog's skin on their back between their two shoulder blades.

Walking dandruff (External)

Walking dandruff also known as Chylidiella is an external parasite that looks like dry skin, however under a microscope it moves and looks like a bug. This type of parasite is not life threatening to a Pomeranian but rather an annoying one to get rid of. The cure over a few month periods is to purchase a bottle of frontline spray from your veterinarian. Using the spray bottle of this medicated formula is more cost affective as you will need more to cover a wider area. Instead of placing a small tube between the shoulder blades, you are going to spray one full squirt per pound of body weight. For instance if your pom weighs 6 pounds, you would administer 6 full sprays from the bottle, covering a wide area of the back. Repeat this routine once every 30 days until your veterinarian tells you otherwise.

Tapeworms (Internal)

Tapeworms are manifested by a dog ingesting a flea. To destroy the diagnosis of tapeworms in your Pomeranian, your vet will administer a one time pill that will take care of the problem. It is a must to provide this one time pill to your pom as tapeworms will not go away otherwise and your pom will eat continuously without weight gain.

Heartworms (Internal)

Heartworms are transmitted through the bite of a mosquito. This parasite can be a life threatening illness, however if detected early most cases are treatable with medication. There are daily supplements that your vet can provide to help prevent a horrible outbreak of heartworms.

Roundworms (Internal)

Roundworms can be permitted through soil if a dog happened to ingest an egg through the dirt, however in most cases roundworms are passed down postnatal from mother to pups. This is an easily treatable parasite as a dewormer called Panacur given one a day for three days will rid your pom from roundworms.

Hookworms (Internal)

Hookworms are another example of an internal parasite. They are also treated with panacur or a similar medication distributed by your veterinarian.

Whipworms (Internal)

Whipworms manifest themselves in the soil and will infect dogs that ingest the eggs through the dirt. This is also cured by Panacur or a similar formula recommended by your veterinarian.

Coccidian (Internal)

Coccidian is an internal parasite that is a little more difficult to destroy. It is quite common in puppies and is usually passed from mother to pups postnatal. The puppies stool has a fouler odor than the other named parasites, yet it can be cured. Albon is the choice of medication administered by veterinarians and is given once a day for 4 to 5 days. Depending on the weight of the puppies, your vet will determine the correct dosage of the medicine per day.

American Kennel Club (AKC) Pomeranian Breed Standard

General Appearance

The Pomeranian is a compact, short-backed, active toy dog. He has a soft, dense undercoat with a profuse harsh-textured outer coat. His heavily plumed tail is set high and lies flat on his back. He is alert in character, exhibits intelligence in expression, is buoyant in deportment, and is inquisitive by nature. The Pomeranian is cocky, commanding, and animated as he gaits. He is sound in composition and action.

Size, Proportion, Substance

The average weight of the Pomeranian is from 3 to 7 pounds, with the ideal weight for the show specimen being 4 to 6 pounds. Any dog over or under the limits is objectionable. However, overall quality is to be favored over size. The distance from the point of the shoulder to the point of the buttocks is slightly shorter than from the highest point of the withers to the ground. The distance from the brisket to the ground is half the height at the withers. He is medium-boned, and the length of his legs is in proportion to a well-balanced frame. When examined, he feels sturdy.

Head

The head is in balance with the body. The muzzle is rather short, straight, fine, free of lippiness and never snipey. His expression is alert and may be referred to as fox-like. The skull is closed. The top of the skull is slightly rounded, but not domed. When viewed from the front and side, one sees small ears which are mounted high and carried erect. To form a wedge, visualize a line from the tip of the nose ascending through the center of the eyes and the tip of the ears. The eyes are dark, bright, medium in size and almond shaped. They are set well into the skull on either side of a well-pronounced stop. The pigmentation is black on the nose and eye rims except self colored is brown, beaver, and blue dogs. The teeth meet in a scissors bite. One tooth out of alignment is acceptable. *Major faults:* Round, domed skull; under-shot mouth; over shot mouth.

Neck, Topline, Body

The neck is short with its base set well into the shoulders to allow the head to be carried high. The back is short with a level topline. The body is compact and well-ribbed with brisket reaching the elbow. The plumed tail is one of the characteristics of the breed, and lies flat and straight on the back.

Forequarters

The Pomeranian has sufficient layback of shoulders to carry the neck and head proud and high. The shoulders and legs are moderately muscled. The length of the shoulder blade and upper arm are equal. The forelegs are straight and parallel to each other. Height from elbows to withers approximately equals height from ground to elbow. The pasterns are straight and strong. The feet are well-arched, compact, and turn neither nor out. He stands well up on his toes. Dewclaws may be removed. *Major Faults:* Down in pasterns.

Hindquarters

The angulation of the hindquarters balances that of the forequarters. The buttocks are well behind the set of the tail. The thighs are moderately muscled with stifles that are moderately bent and clearly defined. The hocks are perpendicular to the ground and the legs are straight and parallel to each other. The feet are well-arched, compact, and turn neither in nor out. He stands well up on his toes. Dewclaws, if any on the hind legs may be removed. Major Faults: Cow hocks of lack of soundness in hind legs or stifles.

Gait. The Pomeranian's gait is smooth, free, balanced and vigorous. He has good reach in his forequarters and strong drive with his hindquarters. Each rear leg moves in line with the foreleg on the same side. To achieve balance, his legs converge slightly inward toward a center line beneath his body. The rear and front legs are thrown neither in nor out. The topline remains level, and his overall balance and outline are maintained.

Coat

A Pomeranian is noted for its double coat. The undercoat is soft and dense. The outer-coat is long, straight, glistening and harsh in texture. A thick undercoat will hold up and permit the guard hair to stand off from the Pomeranian's body. The coat is abundant from the neck and fore part of the shoulders and chest, forming a frill which extends over the shoulders and chest. The head and leg coat is tightly packed and shorter in length than that of the body. The forequarters are well-feathered to the hock. The tail is profusely covered with long, harsh, spreading straight hair. Trimming for neatness and a clean outline is permissible. Major Faults: Soft, flat or open coat.

Color

All colors, patterns, and variations there-of are allowed and must be judged on an equal basis. Patterns: Black and Tan-tan or rust sharply defined, appearing above each eye and on muzzle, throat, and fore chest, on all legs and feet and below the tail. The richer the tan the more desirable. Brindle—the base color is gold, red, or orange-brindled with strong black cross stripes: Parti-color—is white with any other color distributed in patches with a white blaze preferred on the head. Classifications: The open classes at specialty shows may be divided by color as follows: Open Red, Orange, Cream, and Sable; Open Black, Brown, and Blue; Open Any Other Color, Pattern, or Variation.

Temperament

The Pomeranian is an extrovert, exhibiting great intelligence and a vivacious spirit, making him a great companion dog as well as a competitive show dog.

Even though a toy dog, the Pomeranian must be subject to the same requirements of soundness and structure prescribed for all breeds, and any deviation from the ideal described in the standard should be penalized to the extent of the deviation.

Recommended References for the Pomeranian Owner

General Source:
    The American Kennel Club
    P.O. Box 37900
    Raleigh, NC. 27627-7900

Veterinarians:
    Dr. Christine Wilson
    Steele Canyon Vet Clinic
    Jamul, Ca. 91935
    619-669-7274

    Pet Emergency and Specialty Center (PESC)
    5232 Jackson Dr. Suite #105
    La Mesa, Ca. 91941
    619-462-4800

    Animal Internal Medicine
    5610 Kearny Mesa Rd. #B
    San Diego Ca. 92111
    858-560-7778

    Veterinary Surgical Specialists
    5610 Kearny Mesa Rd. #B
    San Diego, Ca. 92111
    858-560-8006

Eye Clinic For Animals
5610 Kearny Mesa Rd.
San Diego, Ca. 92111
858-502-1277

Grooming:
Cece at Steele Canyon Veterinary Clinic
Cece is the BEST dog groomer I have ever met!
Jamul, Ca. 91935
619-669-7274

Petsmart
El Cajon, Ca.
619-442-0600

Petco
Rancho San Diego, Ca.
619-670-9688

Pet Supplies:
Petco
Petsmart
Dr.'s Foster and Smith Catalog

978-0-595-45077-0
0-595-45077-6